JEMMA KENNEDY

Jemma Kennedy's plays include *The Gift*, part of the Hoard Festival for the New Vic Theatre, *The Summer Book* and *The Prince and the Pauper* for the Unicorn Theatre, *The Grand Irrationality* for the Lost Theatre Studio (Los Angeles) and *Don't Feed the Animals* for National Theatre Connections 2013. Jemma was Pearson Playwright at the National Theatre in 2010 and part of the inaugural Soho 6 writing scheme with Soho Theatre Company in 2012. She is currently adapting Barbara Pym's novel *Excellent Women* for BBC Films and her first film *Captain Webb* (Marathon Films, Miramax) is due for release in 2015. Her novel *Skywalking* was published by Penguin/Viking in 2002. Jemma has acted as a writing mentor and judge for the National Theatre's New Views playwriting course and competition for young writers, and teaches playwriting at the National Theatre's Clore Learning Centre. She has also mentored writers for the Koestler Trust.

Other Plays for Young People to Perform from Nick Hern Books

Original Plays

100
Christopher Heimann,
Neil Monaghan, Diene Petterle

BLOOD AND ICE
Liz Lochhead

BOYS
Ella Hickson

BUNNY
Jack Thorne

BURYING YOUR BROTHER IN THE
    PAVEMENT
Jack Thorne

CHRISTMAS IS MILES AWAY
Chloë Moss

COCKROACH
Sam Holcroft

THE DOMINO EFFECT
    AND OTHER PLAYS
Fin Kennedy

DISCO PIGS
Enda Walsh

EIGHT
Ella Hickson

GIRLS LIKE THAT
Evan Placey

HOW TO DISAPPEAR COMPLETELY
    AND NEVER BE FOUND
Fin Kennedy

I CAUGHT CRABS IN
    WALBERSWICK
Joel Horwood

KINDERTRANSPORT
Diane Samuels

MOGADISHU
Vivienne Franzmann

MOTH
Declan Greene

THE MYSTAE
Nick Whitby

OVERSPILL
Ali Taylor

PRONOUN
Evan Placey

SAME
Deborah Bruce

THERE IS A WAR
Tom Basden

THE URBAN GIRL'S GUIDE TO
    CAMPING AND OTHER PLAYS
Fin Kennedy

THE WARDROBE
Sam Holcroft

Adaptations

ANIMAL FARM
Ian Wooldridge
Adapted from George Orwell

ARABIAN NIGHTS
Dominic Cooke

BEAUTY AND THE BEAST
Laurence Boswell

CORAM BOY
Helen Edmundson
Adapted from Jamila Gavin

DAVID COPPERFIELD
Alastair Cording
Adapted from Charles Dickens

GREAT EXPECTATIONS
Nick Ormerod and Declan Donnellan
Adapted from Charles Dickens

HIS DARK MATERIALS
Nicholas Wright
Adapted from Philip Pullman

THE JUNGLE BOOK
Stuart Paterson
Adapted from Rudyard Kipling

KENSUKE'S KINGDOM
Stuart Paterson
Adapted from Michael Morpurgo

KES
Lawrence Till
Adapted from Barry Hines

THE LOTTIE PROJECT
Vicky Ireland
Adapted from Jacqueline Wilson

MIDNIGHT
Vicky Ireland
Adapted from Jacqueline Wilson

NOUGHTS & CROSSES
Dominic Cooke
Adapted from Malorie Blackman

THE RAILWAY CHILDREN
Mike Kenny
Adapted from E. Nesbit

SWALLOWS AND AMAZONS
Helen Edmundson and Neil Hannon
Adapted from Arthur Ransome

TO SIR, WITH LOVE
Ayub Khan-Din
Adapted from E.R Braithwaite

TREASURE ISLAND
Stuart Paterson
Adapted from Robert Louis Stevenson

WENDY & PETER PAN
Ella Hickson
Adapted from J.M. Barrie

THE WOLVES OF WILLOUGHBY
    CHASE
Russ Tunney
Adapted from Joan Aiken

Jemma Kennedy

SECOND PERSON NARRATIVE

NICK HERN BOOKS
www.nickhernbooks.co.uk

TONIC THEATRE
www.tonictheatre.co.uk

A Nick Hern Book

Second Person Narrative first published as a paperback original in Great Britain in 2015 by Nick Hern Books Limited, The Glasshouse, 49a Goldhawk Road, London W12 8QP, in association with Tonic Theatre

Second Person Narrative copyright © 2015 Jemma Kennedy

Jemma Kennedy has asserted her right to be identified as the author of this work

Cover image by Kathy Barber, Bullet Creative, www.bulletcreative.com

Designed and typeset by Nick Hern Books, London
Printed and bound in Great Britain by Mimeo Ltd, Huntingdon, Cambridgeshire PE29 6XX

A CIP catalogue record for this book is available from the British Library

ISBN   978 1 84842 501 9

Woodland
CARBON
www.woodlandcarbon.co.uk
NICK HERN BOOKS
Printed on Carbon Captured paper

Contents

THE LIGHT BURNS BLUE BY SILVA SEMERCIYAN

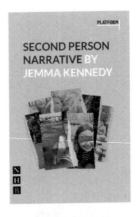

SECOND PERSON NARRATIVE BY JEMMA KENNEDY

THIS CHANGES EVERYTHING BY JOEL HORWOOD

PLATFORM

Commissioning and publishing a range of new plays for young actors which put girls and their stories centre stage is something I have wanted to do for a long time and, since Tonic Theatre was formed in 2011, it is an idea I have been looking to get off the ground. Tonic exists to support UK theatre to achieve greater gender equality in its workforces and its repertoires; essentially our mission is to catalyse a culture-shift in how theatre thinks and works, so that talented women are given the same levels of support and opportunity as talented men.

While it has pretty big aspirations, Tonic is a tiny organisation; we have one-and-a-bit members of staff, no core funding, and a very modest financial turnover. Because we have such limited funds and capacity, we have to use these wisely and consequently are extremely strategic about where we target our efforts. I spend much time looking to identify 'pressure points' – places where, with a bit of work, a far bigger ripple effect can be achieved. For this reason, much of our work to date has been focused on partnerships with some of the largest organisations in the country, because if they change, others will follow. But youth drama has always been clear to me as one of the greatest pressure points of all. It is the engine room of the theatre industry; tomorrow's theatre-makers (not to mention audience members) are to be found today in youth-theatre groups, university drama societies and school drama clubs all over the country.

If we can challenge their assumptions about the role of women's stories, voices, and ideas in drama, then change in the profession – in time – will be immeasurably easier to achieve.

Beyond this strategic interest in youth drama, I was convinced that girls were getting a raw deal and I found that troubling. Having worked previously as a youth-theatre director, I was familiar with the regular challenge of trying to find scripts that had adequate numbers of female roles for all the committed and talented girls that wanted to take part. In nearly all the various youth-drama groups I worked in across a five-year period, there were significantly more girls than boys. However, when it came to finding big-cast, age-appropriate plays for them to work on, I was constantly frustrated by how few there seemed to be that provided enough opportunity for the girls, its most loyal and committed participants. When looking at contemporary new writing for young actors to perform, one could be mistaken for thinking that youth drama was a predominantly male pursuit, rather than the other way round.

Aside from the practicalities of matching the number of roles to the number of girls in any one drama group, the nature of writing for female characters was something I struggled to get excited about. While there were some notable examples, often the writing for female characters seemed somewhat lacklustre. They tended to be characters at the periphery of the action rather than its heart, with far less to say and do than their male counterparts, and with a tendency towards being one-dimensional, rather than complex or vibrant, funny or surprising. Why was it that in the twenty-first century the *quality* as well as the *quantity* of roles being written for girls still seemed to lag behind those for boys so demonstrably?

Keen to check I wasn't just imagining this imbalance, Tonic conducted a nationwide research study looking into opportunities for girls in youth drama, focusing on the quantity *and* quality of roles available to them. The research was written up into a report, *Swimming in the shallow end*, and is published on the Tonic Theatre website. Not only did the research confirm my worst fears – more depressingly, it exceeded them. While many of the research participants were vocal about the social, artistic and emotional benefits that participation in youth-drama productions can have on a young person's life, so too were they – to quote the report – on 'the erosion to self-esteem, confidence and aspiration when these opportunities are repeatedly held out of reach… [and] for too many girls, this is the case'.

But despite the doom and gloom of the research findings, there remained an exciting proposition; to write stories that weren't currently being put on stage, and to foreground – rather than ignore – the experiences, achievements and world-view of young women, perhaps the group above all others in British society whose situation has altered so dramatically and excitingly over the past hundred or so years. Tonic commissioned writers I was most fascinated to see respond to the brief set to them: a large-cast play written specifically for performance by young actors, with mainly or entirely female casts and in which the female characters should be no less complex or challenging than the male characters. I asked them to write in such a way that these plays could be performed by young people anywhere in the country, and that there should be scope for every school, college and youth-theatre group performing the play to make a production their own.

At Tonic our hope is that the first Platform plays, of which this is one, will be just the beginning of a longer trajectory of work for us. Although it entails further fundraising mountains to climb, we plan to commission and publish more plays over future years. Our aspiration is that over time Platform will become a new canon of writing for young actors and one that puts girls and their lives centre stage. I dearly hope that they will be taken up by groups all over the country and performed for many years to come.

Lucy Kerbel
Director, Tonic Theatre

Acknowledgments

Tonic would like to extend its sincere thanks to:

Matt Applewhite, Tamara von Werthern, Jon Barton and all at Nick Hern Books. Moira Buffini, Kendall Masson, Matthew Poxon, Racheli Sternberg, Steph Weller. Arts Council England. The Austin and Hope Pilkington Trust. Anna Niland and the National Youth Theatre of Great Britain. Jennifer Tuckett and Central Saint Martins, Richard Williams and Drama Centre. The National Theatre Studio. English Touring Theatre.

To all the generous donors who have enabled Platform to happen. Above all to Joan Carr, who loved books, delighted in live performance, and who believed girls should never have anything less than boys.

TONIC
THEATRE

Tonic Theatre was created in 2011 as a way of supporting the theatre industry to achieve greater gender equality in its workforces and repertoires. Today, Tonic partners with leading theatre companies around the UK on a range of projects, schemes, and creative works. Our groundbreaking Advance programme (www.tonictheatre-advance.co.uk) saw us work with the artistic directors and senior creative staff of a cohort of England's most influential theatres to bring about concrete change within their own organisations and the wider industry. It is a process the *Guardian* commented 'could transform the theatrical landscape forever'. *100 Great Plays for Women*, our previous collaboration with Nick Hern Books, was published in 2013 to wide acclaim and was subsequently the inspiration for a series of lectures at the National Theatre. We are now delighted to be launching Platform, our range of new plays commissioned to increase opportunity and aspiration among girls and young women who take part in youth drama.

Tonic's approach involves getting to grips with the principles that lie beneath how our industry functions – our working methods, decision-making processes, and organisational structures – and identifying how, in their current form, these can create barriers. Once we have done that, we devise practical yet imaginative alternative approaches and work with our partners to trial and deliver them. Essentially, our goal is to equip our colleagues in UK theatre with the tools they need to ensure a greater level of female talent is able to rise to the top.

Tonic is Affiliate Company at the National Theatre Studio.

www.tonictheatre.co.uk

Nick Hern Books

Theatre publishers & performing rights agents

Here at the Performing Rights Department at Nick Hern Books, we're often asked 'Are there any plays for young people?'... 'Have you got anything for a large cast?'... and 'Is there anything with strong female roles?'

Whilst the answer to these questions is, in each case, a resounding 'Yes!' (and in fact the majority of plays we've published in the last five years have been *by* women), the number of plays that fulfil all three of these criteria – strong roles for a large, predominantly or all-female cast of young actors – is less plentiful. Yet that's where there's so much demand! Nearly every teacher and youth-theatre director in the country knows that it's girls who make up the majority of their casts, and yet the plays available are often dominated by men. Because we can generally only publish what is being produced on the professional stages of the UK, until the theatre industry starts staging more plays with these qualities, the numbers will remain low. It's a vicious circle.

So with Platform, we are delighted to publish and license three plays that give young women good, strong roles to get their teeth into, and that will help them build their self-esteem and confidence in their own skills.

Nick Hern Books look after the amateur performing rights to over a thousand plays, and we know from experience that when it comes to choosing the right play it can be confusing (and pricey) to read enough of what's out there until you know which play is right for you. This is why we send out approval copies: up to three plays at a time, for thirty days, after which they have to be paid for, or returned to us in mint condition and you just need to pay the postage. So there is no reason not to read all three Platform plays to see if they will suit your school, college or youth-theatre group. We're very hopeful that one of them will.

Performing rights to the three plays will be available at a specially reduced rate to enable even those on a very tight budget to perform them. Discounts are also available on cast sets of scripts; and the cover images on these books can be supplied, free of charge, for you to use on your poster.

If you have any questions about Platform, or any of the plays on our list, or want to talk about what you're looking for, we are always happy to speak with you. Call us on 020 8749 4953, or email us at rights@nickhernbooks.co.uk.

Tamara von Werthern
Performing Rights Manager
Nick Hern Books

www.nickhernbooks.co.uk

Introduction

Jemma Kennedy

Once upon a time, etc. A baby girl is born. You. A blank page awaiting a life story. Of course there are some things already scribbled in the margins. The backstory you have inherited from your family. The future story that they have idealised for you. The gendered expectations of your culture. But no matter, you are YOU. The creator of Your Own Unique Narrative™. You will self-author yourself into a girl, then a teenager, a young woman, a middle-aged one, an elderly one with most of your life behind you. You will die, and probably become a backstory for someone else, as yet unborn. The End.

But wait, isn't the heroine always an 'I' – the active subject of a first-person narrative? So how much of you is 'I' and how much is YOU? And aren't there many YOUs? And how does Your Own Unique Narrative™ fit together with the YOUs created for and about you by parents, relatives, friends, teachers, colleagues, lovers? Of course their intentions are honourable. They just want you to be your best YOU. They will expertly advise you how to eat, love, dress, work, behave. They will teach you that you are an individual with the privileges and responsibilities of an 'I' while inviting YOU to become part of a pack, a unit, a network of yous.

You attend a workshop with a playwright who asks you to imagine your future YOU. You know that the end result, the main goal, the reward for your efforts is your happiness. What that is exactly and how you achieve it is still a matter of speculation. You know you have some choice in the matter. But sometimes you feel that those choices are an illusion, created by all the honourable experts. Somewhere along the line you have outgrown the simple narratives of your childhood. You are aware of the gap between the experts' stories about YOU, which are generally either a) depressingly tragic, or b) relentlessly positive, and the random events of your life, the unforeseen accidents, the dead endings. You have an uneasy feeling that things don't always add up like the experts promised. What if you can't author your story the way you want to? What if your story is authoring you?

And wait, where are the stories that reflect this problem? The playwright, who spends her days trying to craft well-behaved dramatic narratives with orderly triggers, twists, crises and moral resolutions, hears the hope and anxiety in your conflicted visions of Your Own Unique Narrative™ . She sees how much is asked of you in the eternal battle between the I and the YOU. She wants you to know how brave you are, how resilient, how ordinary, how special. She would like to write a reassuring play in which your potential is fully realised and you live happily ever after. But her play won't behave. The writer throws her toys out of her pram and writes a series of scenes that do not make up either an a) depressingly tragic, or b) relentlessly positive narrative. YOU are in all of them. She hopes you accept the gesture as one of solidarity.

Acknowledgements

Many thanks to Lucy Kerbel, Anna Niland and all the wonderful actors from the National Youth Theatre who shared their thoughts with me: Seraphina Mary Beh, Charlotte Elvin, Anna Garvey, Natasha Heliotis, Ellie James, Bryony Jarvis Taylor, Lily Lesser, Ayten Manyera, Mia Shurysmith, and Melissa Taylor.

Production Note

The play is intended for a large ensemble group of actors –
minimum seven actors, no maximum. It was written for an all-
female cast but can of course be performed by a mixed
company. The YOU of the play can be played by a single actor
or by several different ones. If it is performed by a very large
company other single characters could be played by multiples
of actors to increase the number of parts.

The more physically constructed the play feels, the better. The
company can make and dismantle scenes as part of the action.
They can carry over props into subsequent scenes. They can
display or speak scene titles and stage directions. They can add
music, voice-over and movement – whatever helps create the
sense of a deliberately assembled narrative.

In certain scenes YOU is not physically present onstage but is
still theatrically engaged with onstage characters. The use of a
short pause indicates that onstage characters are listening to
what YOU is saying. I'd suggest that any theatrical conventions
used to create this 'absent presence' are made consistent
throughout the play.

As each scene shows a linear progression in the life of YOU,
YOU's physical age should be made clear at the beginning of
the scene. For example, displayed on a sign, incorporated into a
prop, or told to the audience directly. However every scene
should be set in the present day.

Each scene contains at least one concrete prop which can all be
brought together in the final scene. You can, of course,
introduce other props into scenes as you wish.

The running order of scenes should be presented as written.

Dialogue in brackets indicates an aside or a peripheral
conversation.

SECOND PERSON NARRATIVE

Characters

YOU
CONSULTANT
MUM
GRANDMOTHER
MAGAZINE
BABYSITTER
TV HE
TV SHE
BOOK
PHOTOGRAPHER
GIRL 1
GIRL 2
GIRL 3
GIRL 4
GIRL 5
AUNT
COUSIN
HIM
FRIEND 1
FRIEND 2
FRIEND 3
FRIEND 4
FRIEND 5
SALESWOMAN
INSTRUCTOR
DAUGHTER
STRANGER
QUESTIONNAIRE
INTERVIEWER
WOMAN 1
WOMAN 2
WOMAN 3

OFFICIALS
MIDWIVES
TEACHERS
FRIENDS
SENIORS
TRAINEES
RELATIVES
FILM EXECUTIVES
CO-WORKERS
EXERCISERS
ESTATE AGENTS

BARTENDER, *non-speaking*
THERAPIST, *non-speaking*

Prologue

A group of OFFICIALS *bring* YOU *on. There's a balloon tied around your wrist.*

OFFICIALS. Off you go then and best of luck

It's bound to be different this time around though some of it might seem familiar

The big questions, we mean

The beginnings, middles, endings, et cetera

Still, not to worry, it's all a work-in-progress

And don't forget you're welcome to draw your own conclusions

Ready?

YOU *nod. An* OFFICIAL *takes out a pin and pops the balloon. A newborn wails.*

PART ONE

Once Upon a Time, etc.

A group of MIDWIVES *are gathered around a bed.*

MIDWIVES. Here she is

A little girl!

Hello you!

Aren't you perfect

And loud – did you hear that?

A real war cry!

'Here I am!'

'You'd all better listen to me!'

Well done Mrs

(Miss

Ms?

Shhh

Is there a father?

Shhh, not now)

Can you believe she'll be an old woman one day

Can you believe one day she'll die of old age

Hopefully – of old age, I mean, not prematurely

Give her a chance, she might be a president

She might be a famous soprano

She might be a scientist who invents a compound that saves the Earth

She might live an averagely happy life without great
ambition or drama

Well

Well

That's not exactly –

Shhh, the consultant's coming

The consultant!

CONSULTANT *enters*.

CONSULTANT. How are we all ladies?

MIDWIVES. Very well thanks

Fine

Tired but fine

Bit emotional actually

We're all absolutely fine

CONSULTANT. Good, then let's get on with it. Weight,
length?

MIDWIVES. Checked

CONSULTANT. Lungs, eyes, heart?

MIDWIVES. Checked

CONSULTANT. Post-partum strategy?

MIDWIVES. Checked

Checked

Checked

CONSULTANT. Hale and healthy, whole life ahead of her,
world, oyster, et cetera. Proceed

MIDWIVES. Yes doctor

CONSULTANT. Clean her up. And don't forget to label her

*Everyone moves away from the bed and leaves. A woman –
your* MUM *– sits up, exhausted. She removes her surgical
cap.*

MUM. Hello? What happens next?

Lucky Girl

You're three, at home with your MUM *and* GRANDMOTHER.
Your MUM *holds a toy rabbit. (*YOU *are not physically present
in the scene.)*

MUM. Well?

GRANDMOTHER. Have you decided to be good or not?

Short pause.

MUM. Let's see what Rabbit has to say about that.

Your MUM *pretends to listen to Rabbit.*

Rabbit says he's sad because you're not behaving.

Short pause.

No he's isn't pretending.

GRANDMOTHER. He's not, listen. Rabbit says – (*Rabbit's
voice.*) I'm very sad you're not behaving.

Short pause.

MUM. That *is* how Rabbit talks, you just heard him talking.

GRANDMOTHER. He's got a sore throat, that's all.

MUM. Yes, and Rabbit says – (*Rabbit's voice.*) if you don't
want your new shoes, I'd be glad to have them.

Short pause.

Of course we understand him, we can speak Rabbit as well, you know.

Short pause.

GRANDMOTHER. We learned at nursery, that's where.

(All these questions

MUM. I know it's exhausting

GRANDMOTHER. But logical, at least

MUM. Yes, there is a logic to it)

Anyway, Rabbit told us –

Short pause.

Fine he can't talk, he wrote it down.

Short pause.

He can, he's a very clever rabbit and he'd love new shoes.

GRANDMOTHER. He would, he'd go to nursery in his new shoes, ever so pleased.

MUM. Lots of children don't even have shoes, they have to walk barefoot.

GRANDMOTHER. Barefoot, dog mess, broken glass, you're a lucky girl.

Short pause.

MUM. No we're not pretending, not about the broken glass, anyway, or do you mean about Rabbit going to nursery?

(She keeps changing the story

GRANDMOTHER. Yes she does, it's infuriating

MUM. Imaginative, at least

GRANDMOTHER. It's certainly imaginative)

Anyway you can wear them and go to nursery or you can stay at home it's your choice.

(MUM. She can't stay at home actually because I have to go to
   work

GRANDMOTHER. And I can't look after her, I have a doctor's
   appointment)

Short pause.

MUM. No you can't stay home alone you're three years old,
   anyway like we said it's your choice.

Short pause.

Oh yes it is young lady.

GRANDMOTHER. You girls today are spoilt with choice,
   when I was a girl we had to be good little girls, we didn't
   have multi-channels and gap years.

MUM. That's right your granny had to fight for women's rights
   while raising a family and doing nursing work.

GRANDMOTHER. So don't tell us you don't have a choice.

Short pause.

MUM. Fine, you didn't choose the shoes. No, or your breakfast.
   Or me, or the nasty curtains or the stupid rabbit, no, fine, you
   didn't choose them either but –

Pause. Your GRANDMOTHER *pretends to listen to the
rabbit.*

GRANDMOTHER (*Rabbit voice*). Perhaps she could wear her
   old shoes, just for today.

The First Big Question

You're five. You're lying on your back looking up at the sky through a pair of binoculars. You're with Rabbit. Rabbit is your best friend.

YOU. Am I God?

YOU *hold Rabbit to your ear and listen to him.*

Because everywhere I go, I'm in charge.

Rabbit talks in your ear again.

Are you sure? Can you prove it?

First Dates

Your teenage BABYSITTER is on the sofa watching TV and reading a celebrity-gossip magazine. She is seventeen.

MAGAZINE. First man to ask her out after

Whisked her off on a private jet to

Cost a reported three million just for

Weighing up her career options while they

YOU *enter. You're seven. You're carrying a storybook.* YOU *read the magazine over the* BABYSITTER*'s shoulder.*

YOU. What's that lady in the bikini doing?

BABYSITTER. Weighing up her career options, what are you doing out of bed?

YOU. I'm not tired. Can I stay up a bit longer?

BABYSITTER. Just for a bit then and don't tell your mum or she won't let me babysit again.

YOU *sit down with your book.* BABYSITTER *reads her magazine.*

MAGAZINE. Romantic waterfront dinner where they

YOU. When's Mum coming back?

BABYSITTER. I don't know, whenever her date's finished.

MAGAZINE. Enjoyed a cocktail beneath the stars and

YOU. Who's she on the date with?

BABYSITTER. A guy from work or someone, apparently he's got a motorbike or something.

MAGAZINE. Blissful night disrupted by manager's

YOU are distracted by the television. The sound of galloping horses and screams.

YOU. Who's that man on the horse with the big stick?

BABYSITTER. I don't know, a Cossack or someone and it's not a stick it's a cutlass or something.

YOU. Why are the peasant girls running away?

BABYSITTER. Not all of them are, see, the pretty one's staying put, she's standing up for them.

You both watch the television.

TV HE. I'm here to liberate you from the Bolsheviks

TV SHE. We may be poor but we don't need liberating, not by you, not by anyone

TV HE. Brave words from a beautiful woman

YOU. Is he going to hurt her?

BABYSITTER. No, he's just pretending to be angry, he actually really likes her.

YOU. But he's tying her to a chair.

BABYSITTER. It's all right he'll fall in love with her and then he'll untie her again.

She goes back to her magazine.

MAGAZINE. Putting career on hold could be a

> Advised to sacrifice her chance of

YOU. What if the date tries to tie Mum to a chair?

BABYSITTER. Don't be silly, he won't do that, not on a first date anyway.

She goes back to her magazine.

MAGAZINE. Second date not planned after

> Fairytale ending unlikely for her

> YOU *look up at the TV.*

TV SHE. You understand nothing about woman, you brute. Nothing!

> YOU *look down at your book.*

BOOK. And in time they came to be king and queen and lived happily ever after.

> YOU *stand up.*

YOU. I'm exhausted. I'm going to back to bed.

A More Rounded View

You're nine. Some TEACHERS *are talking to* YOU *at school. One of the* TEACHERS *is holding a ruler.* (YOU *are not physically present in the scene.*)

TEACHERS. So you're the Cossack, I see

> And you ask your playmates to be peasant girls

> (Pretty peasant girls

> Yes, she's quite specific about the prettiness)

> And they have to weave and bake and clean in their

Hovels

Right, and then you, the Cossack, burst in brandishing this ruler

Cutlass

I see, and then you threaten to

Pillage them

Right, pillage them, unless they fall in love with you

(Did Cossacks use cutlasses?

We're not so concerned about historical accuracy

We're more concerned about the tying of peasant girls to chairs, the brandishing of rulers, et cetera)

Do you know what the word 'pillage' means? Oh – well

Well let's say it's a sort of – (*Foreign accent.*) 'I'll have my wicked way with you if you don't do as I say' type of

(I think Cossacks originate in Russia)

The point is it's not a nice thing to do to anyone

Perhaps it makes you feel powerful

It *is* fun being powerful, but there are other ways to be powerful

Yes like being an adventurer or an explorer in the Amazon or perhaps the North Pole, et cetera

Yes and when a pretend game becomes too rough sometimes somebody can get hurt or frightened

(Actually the other Year Fours seem to love it

The point is that nobody else ever gets to play the Cossack)

So you like playing the Cossack, why's that?

Short pause.

It's simpler? Simpler than

Short pause.

Oh, than being a

Oh

Oh

Oh

Short pause.

Well, sometimes it's good to try different roles

Short pause.

Well, because it means you get a more rounded view

Yes, it's fun to be the victim sometimes as well as the oppressor

Not that we're saying that it's fun to be pillaged

Goodness no being pillaged is NEVER fun, not even if you're pretty, especially not then, oh dear

Besides not all peasant girls are victims, not necessarily

(But these ones are being pillaged

They're victims of unexpected violence, yes, but that's not to say they have no autonomy

I suppose it depends on the historical period

It's not about the historical period, it's about the fact that we have to be careful not to condone violence

Or reinforce gender stereotypes, exactly

Exactly it's our job to encourage positivity and aspiration in our young girls

Wait, so we're telling her it's wrong to be the Cossack because he threatens women but it's okay to be the victim because it's better to be a passive heroine than an active hero?)

Hang on, where did she go?

TEACHERS *look out of the window.*

She's back in the playground, playing Cossacks

Girl Most Likely To

You're twelve, among a group of CLASSMATES. *You're each having your school photograph taken by a* PHOTOGRAPHER.

GIRL 1. I'm eleven. I want to open a nail bar.

PHOTOGRAPHER. That's nice. I bet one day you'll own a whole chain of them. (*A camera flashes.*) Who's next? Hi! Tell me how old you are and what *you'd* like to do when you're bigger.

GIRL 2. I'm eleven. I'd like to be a journalist and win awards at a national level.

PHOTOGRAPHER. Wow, a journalist, aren't you ambitious, well done, I'll look out for you, I'm expecting great things, stand still for me. (*A camera flashes.*) Who's next?

GIRL 3. I'm twelve. I'd like to eliminate all my adult body hair by the time I'm thirty. I'd also quite like to be a successful dog groomer.

PHOTOGRAPHER. That's amazing, the best dog groomer in the country, super-groomer, you'll be amazing. (*A camera flashes.*) Who's next?

GIRL 4. I'm eleven. I don't want to be a mum but I'd love to be a really great grandma.

PHOTOGRAPHER. How lovely and you know you can be whatever you want, so don't let anybody tell you that's not good enough because it IS it's AMAZING! (*A camera flashes.*) Next?

YOU. I'm twelve. I think I'd like to be like an explorer and like save the rainforests and really make a difference to the world.

PHOTOGRAPHER. WOW that's so exciting, aren't you amazing, and what a lovely hair clip, I'll look out for you. (*A camera flashes.*) Who's next?

GIRL 5. I'm nearly twelve. I just want to be happy.

PHOTOGRAPHER. That's wonderful and so positive, can you show your best potentially happy smile for the camera?

GIRL 5 *smiles grudgingly. A camera flashes.*

Wow! That's literally the brightest smile I've ever seen, I can tell you've been practising, amazing, who's next?

PART TWO

Things Get Complicated

You're fourteen, you're with a group of your FRIENDS *in the park.* YOU *pass a bottle of suntan lotion around.*

FRIENDS. So I said what did he say and she said she wouldn't say so I said why not and she said she doesn't want to spread gossip 'cause it always gets back eventually and then she'll look like a cow even though he's the one who said it in the first place

Yeah that makes sense man

Yeah man

Wait, look up!

Here it comes

YOU. Woo!

FRIENDS. Vitamin D man!

Pass the lotion

Can't wait for the holidays man!

Goodbye Year Ten

YOU. *Adios numero diez*

FRIENDS. We're gonna party hard this summer

We'll be party central

ALL. Party!

FRIENDS. We'll swoop in and take over the town

Yeah like a load of batshit party vampires!

Do what we want, wear what we want

See who we want, eat what we want

ALL. PARTY!

Laughter.

YOU. Actually I might get a summer job

FRIENDS. What? Don't you want to party?

'Cause we're all gonna party all summer

Party!

YOU. Course I want to party but if I'm gonna party I need like money

FRIENDS. You don't need that much money

Yeah work's boring, man

Yeah you gotta be independent man, you gotta party when you want

YOU. If I want to be independent I have to get a job otherwise I have to like wait for my pocket money and I don't get much

FRIENDS. But then you'll have money and we won't

Yeah and then you'll be like trying to tell *us* when we can party

Yeah and we should be able to do whatever we want whenever we want

Like have the stuff we want, live where we want

Be in relationships we want, have kids when we want

YOU. I don't know if I want kids

FRIENDS. Why not?

We're all having kids

Right, so we can be together like all the time, have kids' parties and stuff

Party! Sorry

YOU. I'd rather travel than have kids, that's all I'm saying

FRIENDS. You might change your mind

> Yeah because every seven years your entire body regenerates itself

> What even your organs?

> Yeah so by the time you're twenty-one you could have like entirely regenerated and become a completely different person

> And then you might want to party with us again and have kids together

YOU. I don't want to be a different person and I do want to party with you I just want a summer job so I can earn some money

FRIENDS. But we do things on our terms not anyone else's

> Yeah like jobs we want or don't want, houses we want

> Kids if we want them, meaningful relationship, organs, parties

> Parties! Sorry

> Just live our lives the way we want to

> Have it all

> The End

> *Pause.*

YOU. You do know you can't have it all any more

FRIENDS. Why not?

YOU. They proved it doesn't work

FRIENDS. Really?

YOU. Yeah. It's a myth, that's what my mum says

> *Pause.*

FRIENDS. So what, you can have

What some of it?

But not all of the time

YOU. Yeah

FRIENDS. So how do you know which things you want are the ones you can have?

And when?

Silence.

Sun's gone in again

I'm freezing man

Shall we go down the shops?

The New Androgyny

Some SENIOR SALES ASSISTANTS *instruct a group of* TRAINEE SALES ASSISTANTS *on the shop floor of a young-fashion retailer.* YOU *are among the trainees. You're sixteen. Energetic music plays.*

SENIORS. Right, to recap: trousers and tops on the table

Hoodies on special at the aisle end

Everyone with us so far?

TRAINEES. Yes

SENIORS. We can't hear you!

TRAINEES. YES!

SENIORS. Good, now don't make the piles too neat, *you* like to handle things when *you* shop, don't you?

TRAINEES. Yes

SENIORS. That's right, you want to feel part of the experience

It's emotional, it's unconscious, it's personal

It's visual, it's about belonging, it's tribal

So let's talk you through the look, okay?

TRAINEES. OKAY

A SENIOR *picks up a jacket and shows it to everyone.*

SENIORS. So this season is about utilitarian luxe

It's comfortable, it communicates strength and power

It's gender neutral, age neutral

It's about attitude, not labels

Head office are calling it the new androgyny

Everyone got that, individually?

TRAINEES. Yes

SENIORS. Are you sure?

TRAINEES. YES!

SENIORS. Floor plan – now, if you're our teen customer, you'll enter over there

You'll probably be with your mother and if so your mother will probably be feeling a bit neurotic

A combination of the static and what she will perceive as the diabolical pumping music

Music that you, her daughter, loves and knows most of the lyrics to, at the very least, the chorus

Everyone sings a bit of the chorus from the energetic song that's playing.

Now your job is to engage the daughter, our young customer

Who is you

Yes, figuratively speaking, to engage yourself

So why not start with a smile at the customer

That's right, why not give her –

Yourself

Give yourself a smile of solidarity

Everyone do that now, let's practise on each other

YOU *and the other* TRAINEES *attempt to give each other smiles of solidarity.*

Good, show her that you understand her –

Your

Your teenage behaviour, *your* tastes, *your* choices, et cetera

Because you are the daughter's new tribe, right here, unfolding the overly neat piles and rehanging this jacket

Working at your first Saturday job while your friends are at home or out having fun

Showing your independence, your determination

Saving up for on-trend new clothes and semi-alcoholic coolers

Expressing your individuality while feeling part of a retail community

Knowing you'd both feel even more yourselves while wearing this new-season imitation-combat jacket with adjustable-sleeving detail

You would all wear it, wouldn't you?

TRAINEES. Yes

SENIORS. Wouldn't you?

TRAINEES. YES!

YOU *put up your hand.*

YOU. Excuse me

SENIORS. Yes?

YOU. What if you don't drink and you buy most of your clothes from charity shops?

Beat.

SENIORS. There'll be time for questions at the end, right now we need to move on

That's right. Everyone with us so far, individually?

TRAINEES. Yes!

SENIORS. Can't hear you

TRAINEES. YES!

The Second Big Question

You're seventeen. You're with your GRANDMOTHER, *who is half-asleep.* YOU *are painting her fingernails with nail polish in an inappropriate shade.*

YOU. Nana? If you spend too much time pretending to be someone else, can you forget who you actually are?

YOU *blow on her fingernails.*

And can anyone tell the difference?

Your GRANDMOTHER *opens her eyes.*

GRANDMOTHER. Who's that there? I don't recognise your voice, love.

The Keys to the Door

You're twenty-one, you're having a family dinner in a restaurant to celebrate your birthday with your MUM, *an* AUNT, *a* TEENAGE COUSIN *and some much older* RELATIVES. *Your boyfriend is outside having a cigarette.*

AUNT. He seems nice

YOU. Do you think so? I think so

AUNT. Very nice, don't you think so?

COUSIN. Yeah he's amazing, did you see his shoes? (*Hiccups.*)

RELATIVES. Is there any more bread there?

Yes we're starving

Yes he's got quite an appetite hasn't he?

MUM. You didn't tell me he was a smoker either

YOU. He's trying to give up

MUM. Really, and he couldn't wait till after we've eaten?

YOU. He's nervous, it's the first time he's met everyone

RELATIVES. I'd be nervous, meeting all you ladies together

COUSIN. We're no ladies – (*Giggles, hiccups.*) Sorry

RELATIVES. Where's that waitress, do you think she'll bring us more bread?

Someone needs something to soak up all the birthday girl's champagne, shall we see if there's any left?

ALL. Happy birthday!

MUM. Someone else seemed to have quite a taste for it too

YOU. (He's nervous, I told you

MUM. He didn't seem nervous, just thirsty

YOU. It's not real champagne anyway, it's only Cava)

RELATIVES. Twenty-one, eh

    The key to the door

COUSIN. I want a key too, and a door, it's not fair – (*Hiccups.*)
Sorry

AUNT. Tell me what he does for a job again?

YOU. Nothing yet, he's looking obviously but it's hard right
now

RELATIVES. I don't envy your generation, no homes, no jobs,
no savings

COUSIN. We don't envy yours; no teeth, no fun, no
boyfriends – (*Giggles, hiccups.*)

AUNT. And did he get you something nice for your birthday?

YOU. Flowers

AUNT. That's sweet

MUM. From the all-night petrol station

    COUSIN *hiccups.*

YOU. It wasn't just flowers

MUM. No, there was the set of toiletries

AUNT. That sounds nice

MUM. Complimentary ones in little plastic bottles pinched
from some bargain chain hotel

    COUSIN *hiccups, giggles.*

RELATIVES. Oh you don't want that

    No you want a cosy B&B in a nice cathedral town

COUSIN. She wouldn't be caught dead in a cathedral town –
(*Hiccups.*) he should take her to Ibiza

YOU. He can't afford it, he can't help it if he isn't working

MUM. So how will he pay rent?

AUNT. You're moving in together?

MUM. That's the plan apparently

COUSIN. Are you, cool! (*Hiccups, giggles.*) Sorry

YOU. We'll get somewhere cheap, I'll pay till he finds work

RELATIVES. What did I say, the key to the door!

MUM. The door of some grubby set of rooms above a discount-wallpaper shop

COUSIN. I'll come and visit you! (*Hiccups.*)

RELATIVES. (Someone needs to give her a fright

Where is that waitress for goodness' sake?)

AUNT. She's twenty-one now, she wants her independence

ALL. Happy birthday!

MUM. Does it have to be with a codependent unemployed chain-smoker she's known for a whole two months?

YOU. Two and a half and so what if he smokes and drinks and doesn't have a job and buys flowers from petrol stations, so what, I love him

MUM. *I* love you, I want what's best for you and it's not him

YOU. How do you know, you went out with some total losers in your day

MUM. Like who?

YOU. The one with the motorbike, he smoked, even his dog smoked

AUNT. I remember the motorbike man

COUSIN. Motorbikes are cool! (*Hiccups.*)

MUM. That was years ago, don't turn the past into a drama

YOU. Don't turn my future into a tragedy. It's my life, it's my door, it's my key, where the hell is he?

RELATIVES. There he is, he's outside, still smoking

> Oh yes, he's talking to the waitress

> Oh yes. Oh, they're swapping numbers, look

> *Everyone looks. Pause.*

YOU. He's a very friendly person

MUM. It looks like it

COUSIN. If you don't want him, I'll have him – (*Giggles.*) My
hiccups have gone. Cool!

Person Specification

*You're twenty-three. YOU are rehearsing for a job interview.
YOU clutch a pile of printed CVs. All of them are your own,
written in different styles.*

YOU (*decisively*). Curriculum Vitae. I am twenty-three. Career
oriented. Decisive. Efficient. Always to the point. Full stop.

> YOU *look at another CV.*

> (*Brightly.*) About Me. I'm twenty-three years of age and I'm
> a fun, energetic, highly motivated team-player with many
> interesting hobbies and a full social life.

> YOU *look at another CV.*

> (*Thoughtfully.*) Personal Statement. At almost twenty-four
> years old I consider myself to be a mature and thoughtful
> individual who cares deeply about the environment. I am a
> Pisces but work equally well with other non-water signs.

> YOU *look at another CV.*

> (*Theatrically.*) CV SOS. Twenty-three-years-young Girl
> Friday seeks Robinson Crusoe to give her sea legs and save
> her from the corporate pirates.

YOU *screw the CVs into a ball and throw them away.*

(*In a normal voice.*) I am an eminently normal person with good and bad qualities and very little experience… I just really really want this job.

Short pause.

You do? You are? (*Big smile.*) Really?

PART THREE

Pivotal Moments

You're twenty-six. You're in a hotel room with a new
BOYFRIEND. *You're packing your backpack. He is reading*
out a hotel review that he's written on a laptop or phone.

HIM. Our room was spacious, the bed very comfortable. The
bathroom was well appointed with complimentary toiletries.

YOU. It's a shame we didn't get to see the cathedral.

HIM. The overhead shower had separate controls which
delivered a good flow-rate with an adjustable temperature.

YOU. You should make a note that they're doing restoration
work.

HIM. The hallways and communal spaces were well kept and
freshly vacuumed.

YOU. Not that it stopped the tourists from filming the
scaffolding.

HIM. The hotel menu changes daily and we had a varied choice
of starters and main courses, including a vegetarian option.

YOU. It's weird, don't you think, like it's not enough to see
with our eyes any more, we need evidence to like
authenticate our experiences or something.

HIM. The dining-room staff were attentive but discreet and
delivered excellent service.

YOU. Personally I find it sad, I don't know why, I just find it –

HIM. Any additional supplements were clearly stated on the
menu card.

YOU *start to talk a bit louder. So does he.*

YOU. Maybe we're in their footage, me watching them, you with your guidebook, maybe they'll wonder who we are, if we're enjoying ourselves, do we love each other

HIM. At breakfast we were presented with a 'help-yourself buffet' of cereals, cheese, cold meats, fresh and preserved fruits, teas and coffees

YOU. Or maybe we'll just look so boring they won't bother.

HIM. Two things; I did ask a member of staff for more information about the hot alternative 'Full English'.

YOU. I'm leaving you.

HIM. But she walked off and did not come back with the answer.

YOU. Did you hear what I said?

HIM. I would also say that the background music in the dining room was a little overbearing.

YOU. I want more than this, I'm going to be thirty in four years and I want I want I don't know to do something extraordinary with my life.

YOU *pick up the backpack and leave.*

HIM. It meant I couldn't digest properly. For those two reasons I'd give the hotel three out of five stars.

Speaking Out

You're twenty-nine. You're receiving an award at an awards ceremony. You're holding a bouquet of flowers.

YOU. Thank you. Thank you so much. It's such an honour to be here... I'm shaking, look at me... anyway, I'm so proud to be receiving the Young Woman of the Year Under Thirty Flawless Finish Everyday Foundation Award. I honestly don't think I did anything that anybody else wouldn't have done... I just saw something happening that I thought was wrong and I decided to... oh, sorry, I think I've got to finish... just to say, quickly, that all I did was speak up and raise my voice and encourage other women to raise their voices and –

Music floods in and cuts YOU *off mid-speech.*

The Story of All Young Women

A group of FILM EXECUTIVES *are having a breakfast meeting. Some of them are reading out an email on a laptop or phone, others listen. (*YOU *are not physically present in the scene.)*

EXECUTIVES. So here's what we sent her three days ago:

'Recently we saw your interview'

(The thing on YouTube?

The interview a couple of years back after she won the award, it's really good

It is, it's really good)

'We saw your interview and we really connected with your story'

'We found it totally universal and yet completely unique'

'It's a story for everyone, but especially for a young female audience with dreams but ordinary limitations'

(So far so good

Exactly, it's positive but respectful, not overly familiar)

'We were also inspired by the fact that you are still so young'

(Youngish, she's thirty-two

Youngish enough to have the bulk of her life still ahead of her)

'Still so young, which makes your actions accessible to our audience'

(Right, there's a realness to her, a sort of normalcy)

'And we really feel that many other young women could connect with you'

(That's nice)

'Because your story is the story of all young women'

'Except in your case you made a stand'

(And of course she's almost beautiful

D'you think so?

She could be made almost beautiful)

'You made a stand and spoke up for others'

(Right, and we watched, the world watched, and we fell in love with her

Right, she overcame enormous personal obstacles, she almost lost everything but she kept her integrity and went on to change the world in a small but significant way

Hang on are we talking about the real girl here or our version?)

'Anyway, just to say once again that we really connected with the beautiful and unique universality of your story'

(Personally I never get involved unless I really connect with the material at a deep emotional level

Absolutely otherwise we wouldn't be able to do our job properly)

'And we feel it is a story that has real potential as a film for television or even possibly cinema'

'We do hope you can come in for a breakfast meeting to discuss our ideas further'

Yada yada yada

That's what we sent her three days ago, CC'd to development

(You didn't CC me

Didn't I? Maybe it was a BCC)

Anyway well done

I think she'll be moved by it

Absolutely, let's wait to see when she can do the breakfast meeting and then we can meet to discuss it before it happens

At breakfast?

Naturally

Another EXECUTIVE *enters.*

We've just heard back from her, she's not coming in for a breakfast meeting

She's not coming in?

What do you mean?

She said she was flattered but she didn't want to have her life turned into a film for television or even possibly cinema

Oh

Oh

Pause.

Well then she's missing out on a really good opportunity

Right, to send out a positive message about female empowerment

It's actually quite irresponsible of her

Yes, what about all those girls out there, the ones who aren't almost beautiful, the ones who are never given a platform?

Girls who might be positively influenced by her story?

Right, who speaks for them?

That's the problem with this generation, they're just so selfish, it's a tragedy really

Pause.

Who wants to try the fruit plate?

Or a pastry. They're really good

They are, they're really good

The Third Big Question

You're thirty-three. You're having a quiet word with yourself in the bathroom mirror as YOU *prepare to apply mascara.*

YOU. You've made the right decision.

> YOU *apply mascara to one eye.*

> You know exactly who you are.

> YOU *apply mascara to the other eye.*

> You have a clear vision for your future.

> *Pause.*

> Right?

Taking Stock

You're thirty-six. You're with a group of FRIENDS *having a group photograph taken.*

FRIENDS. Where should we stand?

   Just in a huddle or in rows?

YOU. Why are you asking me?

FRIEND 1. You were always the one who took charge, that's why.

YOU. No I wasn't.

FRIENDS. You were, remember years ago, that game you invented?

   You used to make us pretend to be peasants.

   You were terrifying, it was great.

YOU. God don't, I feel old.

FRIENDS. We're not old, we're only halfway through.

   Yeah this is just the interval, we're still taking stock.

   Let's get on with it then, why don't we all just stand where we're comfortable.

   Hey, everyone, remember the school photo? 'I'm twelve, I want to be a journalist.'

ALL. AMAZING!

FRIEND 2. How about, I'm thirty-six, I'm assistant political editor and sometimes I just want to read a gossip magazine until I fall asleep with boredom.

   Applause, cheers.

FRIEND 1. How about, I'm thirty-seven, I'm self-employed, I'm secretly addicted to scratching off my nail varnish with a cocktail stick.

   Applause, cheers.

YOU. Okay, I'm thirty-six, I got to visit a rainforest and it was a massive let-down, I got really sick and I hated the food.

Applause, cheers.

FRIEND 4. My turn, I'm thirty-six, I chose not to have kids and that was absolutely the right decision, even though people insisted on feeling sorry for me.

Applause, boos.

FRIEND 3. I'm thirty-seven, I didn't epilate today, I just couldn't be bothered, plus I had to shampoo a labradoodle.

Applause, cheers.

FRIEND 5. I'm nearly thirty-seven, I've given up on finding a concrete reason for my general failure to be happy.

ALL. Ahhhh.

FRIEND 5. Actually it's really liberating when you realise you don't have to fulfil all your potential.

Applause, cheers.

YOU. Are we ready then?

Someone sets up a camera on self-timer. You all huddle together and pose.

FRIENDS. Everyone say cheese.

No, say Cossacks.

ALL. Cossacks!

A flash pops.

PART FOUR

Maximum Confusion

You're thirty-nine. You're shopping with your MUM *in a ladieswear department. She's in her late sixties.*

YOU. What about this, this is nice.

MUM. I really don't need anything, thanks.

YOU. I know but I want to buy you something nice.

MUM. Spend it on yourself, I'm fine.

A SALESWOMAN *enters.*

SALESWOMAN. Can I help you with anything?

MUM. No thank you.

YOU. Actually we're looking for something for my mum.

MUM. Right-o, what sort of occasion?

YOU. I don't know, Mum, do you want something dressy or more everyday?

MUM. I don't need anything, really.

SALESWOMAN. It's never about need, though, is it madam, we try to ban the word need on this floor, let's leave need to the uniforms and shapewear departments. (*Laughs.*)

MUM. Thank you, I'm not in the market for anything today (don't bully me.)

YOU. I'm not bullying you, I want to make you happy, this lady here wants to make you happy, God what's wrong with you?

SALESWOMAN. Shall I pop back in a bit?

MUM. Yes, thank you.

SALESWOMAN *leaves.*

MUM. Forget about me, why don't we get you something for your interview?

YOU. I don't need anything for the interview.

MUM. Do you have to wear a skirt for that sort of interview?

YOU. No Mum, it's not the 1950s.

MUM. I know it's not the 1950s, it hasn't stopped you from wearing skirts. Funny really, you used to be so androgynous, hoodies and jeans all the time.

YOU. That was years ago, I find skirts more appealing now I'm in my thirties.

MUM. Late thirties.

YOU. Whatever, the point is if I do wear a skirt to my interview it's because I like wearing skirts not because I have to.

SALESWOMAN *enters again.*

SALESWOMAN. How are we doing?

YOU. Fine, I'm just explaining to my mother that wearing a skirt doesn't mean you're betraying the female race.

SALESWOMAN. Oh absolutely, skirts are very big this season, head office are calling it the new femininity.

YOU. You see Mum, head office understand that it's okay to dress like a woman and enjoy it. So will my interviewers, who picked out my CV from hundreds of candidates, because not only am I fully qualified in my field I have rounded experience, I have travelled, I've won Young Woman of the Year Awards –

SALESWOMAN. Skirts are actually very empowering, especially with a block heel for contrast.

MUM. This is the new femininity? I see.

YOU. Don't pretend you either know or care about fashion.

SALESWOMAN. Why don't I pull out some items and pop back?

SALESWOMAN *leaves*.

MUM. That was a nice thing to say.

YOU. I'm trying to be nice, I want to buy you something nice but you won't let me.

MUM. Try dressing when you're my age, you can't show your legs, arms, chest, you may as well just wear a sheet with a hole cut out for the head and have done with it.

YOU. Who says you can't show your legs or your arms or your chest?

MUM. Nobody wants to see an old woman's crêpey flesh, call it the new femininity if you like, I call it the same old shite.

YOU. Mum! I'm sorry... why didn't you tell me you felt this way before?

MUM. Because I'm trying to protect you, because that's my job, because I don't want to fill you with fear about getting older and I care more about that than about betraying the female race.

SALESWOMAN *enters*.

SALESWOMAN. I've brought you our best-selling skirts, and for your mother we have some lovely full-length caftans just in, they'll hide a multitude of sins. Is this a bad moment?

You Are Not Alone

You're forty-one. You're at work, in the boardroom, with a group of CO-WORKERS. YOU *are busy unwrapping a very elaborately gift-wrapped parcel.*

CO-WORKERS. We're thrilled for you

We are, really thrilled

YOU. Thanks

CO-WORKERS. Yes it's wonderful news, we knew you were trying

(Did we?

Yes we did) we're just glad it was all relatively straightforward

Well, we don't know that, but we hope it wasn't, you know

It's happened now, anyway, and that's great

It's a good age for it, forty, forty-one

(We don't know that either

She's forty-one, it's on file)

And you obviously really wanted this, so that's great

YOU. Thanks, yes

YOU *are still very occupied with the parcel.*

CO-WORKERS. Of course we'll be sorry to see you go

We will, you've been a real asset to the company

(She's still here, under contract, let's not get ahead of ourselves)

But don't forget we've all been through this already

(I haven't)

Most of us have, and we're here to support you, even if you decide not to come back

That's entirely your decision, and you shouldn't rush in
to it

Of course you'll be bombarded with advice, experts,
pundits

Friends and family, all telling you if you should come back
or not and how and when

Just ignore all the advice

Except ours of course

Because we've been through it and we want you to know
you're not alone

(She's not alone, is she, she's got a partner

We don't know that, let's not make assumptions)

Assuming you've got a partner, which we hope you have

Not that not having a partner isn't in any way abnormal these
days

No, obviously not, but for the sake of argument if you have
got a partner, even then you can feel alone

Yes especially late at night when everyone else is sleeping

Or even in the middle of the day, sitting on the sofa

When it's just you and it, you know

And everybody's rushing around outside, having
appointments, grabbing lunches

And you really feel the isolation of this exclusive longed-for
intimacy

And you look down at it and you think, is it what I thought it
would be like, that life-altering love I wanted to feel so badly
because everyone told me it was the most profound feeling
I'd ever feel, and has it, has it

Has it make me less or more lonely then I was before?

YOU *finally finish unwrapping the parcel.* YOU *remove a set of baby clothes.*

YOU. Thanks!

CO-WORKERS. Neutral colours

We assume you don't know yet

Or don't want to know

(We don't know that, she might want to, lots of people do)

Either way, we got something neutral

YOU. Thanks, it's

CO-WORKERS. We just wanted to let you know that we know what you're about to go through

(Most of us)

And that we'll be here cheering you on from the sidelines

Whatever you decide to do about coming back

(Or not)

Yes, cheering you on from the office

Here in the same old boring meeting room

Busy

Working

Everybody Needs a Special Someone

You're forty-four. You're talking to your child, who is three. You're holding your Rabbit and a sippy cup. (The child is not present in the scene.)

YOU. See this rabbit? He was mine when I was three.

Short pause.

I was once. It was a long time ago now.

Short pause.

Yes, as little as you. Granny gave him to me you see.

Short pause.

Yes Granny who just – yes. Poor old Granny. So this is Rabbit and now I'd like you to have him.

Short pause.

Because it's time he was looked after by someone special.

Short pause.

You. You're special. You're my special –

Short pause.

Oh. Are you sure?

Short pause.

I'll wash him, he's been in a box, you see, waiting for you.

Short pause.

But he's such a sweet little thing, he just wants to be loved and everybody needs a special someone, wait, he wants to say something.

YOU *pretend to listen to the rabbit.*

Rabbit says – *(Rabbit voice.)* I'd love you to be my special someone.

Short pause.

Why are you laughing?

Short pause.

It's not a funny voice, it's Rabbit's voice, anyway I think he's got a cold.

Short pause.

Look please take him, I want you to, otherwise he'll be lonely. Rabbit just wants someone to talk to again. It can't all be over for Rabbit yet.

Rewriting Your Story

You're forty-eight. You're in a dance exercise class with some WOMEN *that* YOU *don't know very well. The* INSTRUCTOR *talks you through in time to the music.*

INSTRUCTOR. Take it left

Take it right

Make it big

Keep it tight

Move those hips

Don't be shy

Shake it out

Now freestyle!

The WOMEN *in the class dance freestyle.* YOU *try to keep up. The* INSTRUCTOR *moves among the class watching everyone individually. She keeps talking in time to the music.*

Show me your moves (yeah!)

Rewrite your story (much better)

Make it good (uh-huh)

DAUGHTER. WHY ARE YOU SO SELFISH, IT DOESN'T EVEN FIT YOU, YOU'VE HAD YOUR TIME, IT'S MY TIME NOW AND YES YOU'RE RIGHT THERE IS ABSOLUTELY NO MYSTERY TO YOU NO WONDER DAD LEFT!

DAUGHTER *removes the black top, throws it on the floor and exits again.*

YOU. You look at your friends. You feel embarrassed. You pick your black top off the floor and wonder if you can actually still get into it

FRIENDS. Why is she talking like that?

Mona Lisa

You're fifty-seven, sitting at a bar drinking a cocktail. A BARTENDER *tends bar. An attractive* STRANGER *smiles at* YOU. YOU *smile back, enigmatically.*

STRANGER. Hi.

YOU. Hi.

STRANGER. I hope you don't mind…

YOU. Why should I mind?

STRANGER. No reason really, you did just smile at me, didn't you?

YOU *smile at the* STRANGER *again.*

Yes, just like that. You looked a bit, I don't know –

YOU. Enigmatic?

STRANGER. Yes, exactly, like the famous painting. (*Laughs.*) I thought I'd come over and say hello.

YOU *smile at the* STRANGER *again.*

Cos if I like it (I like it)

I'll invite you

To join my party

And what kind of music

D'you wanna hear at my party?

YOU *stop dancing, exhausted. The* INSTRUCTOR *passes* YOU *a towel. She addresses the class. They keep dancing.*

D'you wanna hear about tiredness?

ALL. No!

INSTRUCTOR. D'you wanna hear about boredom?

ALL. No!

INSTRUCTOR. D'you wanna hear about divorce?

ALL. No!

INSTRUCTOR. D'you want hear about the menopause?

ALL. No!

YOU *try to start dancing again.*

INSTRUCTOR. We wanna hear about youth

ALL. Youth!

INSTRUCTOR. We wanna hear about fitness

ALL. Fitness!

INSTRUCTOR. We wanna hear about power

ALL. Power!

INSTRUCTOR. We wanna hear positivity

ALL. Positivity!

YOU *collapse. The other* EXERCISERS *help* YOU *up. The* INSTRUCTOR *stops the music.*

INSTRUCTOR. Well done everyone. Let's take five and then work on our 'fifty is the new forty' routine.

Nobody Cares What You're Wearing

You're fifty-six, at home with a group of FRIENDS *who are in your book group.*

FRIENDS. I really enjoyed it, I thought the, what d'you call it, the second-person thingy

Second-person narrative

Yeah I thought that was interesting

It felt a bit weird to me, you're told what to feel and think all the time, it's a bit like being bullied

Your TEENAGE DAUGHTER *enters.*

DAUGHTER. Mum where's my top?

YOU. Which top?

DAUGHTER. The black one, you said you washed it

YOU. I don't know, look in the airing cupboard

DAUGHTER. I did, it's not there

YOU. Well if it went in the basket it got washed and if it got washed it's in the cupboard

DAUGHTER. It's not in either of those places

YOU. Then you've put it somewhere else, I can't help you

DAUGHTER. Why is everything always my fault!

Your DAUGHTER *leaves.*

YOU. Sorry about that. I thought that the point of second-person narrative was to make you identify more with the heroine

FRIENDS. It's hard to identify with her when you're forced to *be* her, what if you don't like her?

I liked trying to identify with her, I found her sort of enigmatic

Women aren't enigmatic though, not unless they're in a French film, not when you get to our age

Your DAUGHTER *enters again.*

DAUGHTER. Can I borrow your black top? The one that's too small for you

YOU. It's not too small for me

DAUGHTER. Whatever I need a black top to go with these trousers, okay?

YOU. Actually I was going to wear it tomorrow

DAUGHTER. It's for my date, all right, I'm going on a date, I told you, it's important

YOU. How do you know I'm not going on a date tomorrow?

DAUGHTER. I'm not joking, Mum, you're fifty-six, nobody cares what you're wearing

DAUGHTER *exits.*

FRIENDS. You're not really going on a date, are you?

YOU. Of course I'm not

FRIENDS. Why 'of course?' You could easily go on a date if you wanted

YOU. Maybe she's right, who's interested in a woman my age with no mystery to her and clothes that don't fit?

DAUGHTER *enters wearing the black top.*

DAUGHTER. I'm going out now, I'm wearing the black top, okay?

YOU. No it's not okay it's rude to keep interrupting us like this I don't like the way you're talking to me for goodness' sake the world's not going to end if you don't wear my black top	DAUGHTER. Well tough I'm wearing it you're just trying to spoil everything I need it more than you you're not even busy you're just sitting around talking who even reads books any more

YOU. Right take it off please, right now

I don't think I've seen you here before.

YOU. Maybe not.

STRANGER. Are you local?

YOU. I wouldn't like to say.

STRANGER. So what brought you to this neighbourhood tonight?

YOU *shrug mysteriously.*

YOU. Who knows?

STRANGER. Very mysterious. (*Laughs.*) Do you work around here perhaps?

YOU *shake your head.* YOU *sip your drink enigmatically.*

Making me work for it, eh? (*Laughs.*) What's that you're drinking?

YOU. Guess.

STRANGER. Oh, er, it looks like a cocktail…

YOU. It might be.

STRANGER. Is it nice?

YOU. I haven't made up my mind yet.

STRANGER. Right. Can I ask you your name?

YOU. You can ask… but I never give too much away on a first meeting.

STRANGER. Oh, right. (*Pause.*) If you'll excuse me. I think I need the toilet.

The STRANGER *gets up and leaves.* YOU *sit there for a moment.* YOU *drain your glass.* YOU *address the* BARTENDER.

YOU. Can I try something different please?

The Fourth Big Question

You're fifty-nine. You're having a session with your
THERAPIST.

YOU. I just want to know why I feel like a minor character in
the story of my own life.

Your THERAPIST *makes a note in her notepad. Pause.*

You want me to answer that myself, don't you?

PART FIVE

The Final Outcome

You're sixty. You're at home filling out a questionnaire.

QUESTIONNAIRE. Congratulations on reaching sixty and qualifying for your Free Pass. Please fill out the enclosed questionnaire for further advice on how to make the most of your retirement years.

Are you still physically active?

Do you have regular aches and pains?

Do you often forget the names of friends and family?

Are you happier in the countryside than in a city?

Do you have a pet?

Do you ever speak to the pet in the same infantile voice you once used on your children?

Do you ever experience feelings of inherent distrust in professional tradespeople who speak with a foreign accent?

Have you ever considered what song you would like to have played at your funeral?

Or is it in fact a piece of classical music?

Do you know the correct pronunciation of the words: a) inchoate b) haemorrhoids c) telegram.

Would you rather die a) surrounded by friends and family b) under the care of privately trained professionals or c) in a cheap hotel after a one-night stand with a stranger.

Are you as old as you feel or as young as you look? And which is better?

Now add up your score.

YOU *add up your score.*

YOU. Group four. You are definitely showing your age. But
don't worry. Taking up a hobby or creative pursuit can help
stave off boredom and mental stagnation. It is also quite
possible that you lied about some of your answers.

Hotel With One Star

*You're sixty-five, you've just finished reading some of your
poems at a poetry recital.*

INTERVIEWER. Your debut collection has been praised for its
authenticity of its older female voice, is that important to
you?

YOU. Well yes, as much as I want my readers to be able to
relate to what I say.

INTERVIEWER. Shall we talk about the titular poem in *your*
collection –

YOU. 'Hotel With One Star'?

INTERVIEWER. Yes, about the sixty-five-year-old woman who
dies of a heart attack in a, well, in a hotel with one star.
Perhaps let's open it up to the audience. Anyone? Yes, eager
woman over there with her hand up.

WOMAN 1. If I may start by quoting from my favourite stanza:
(*Reads from your poetry book.*) 'She awakes to the clang of a
radiator dawn / Beside the ageing salesman with the thinning
hair / Who last night had pressed her to try the steak / As if
he knew it would be her last supper.'

INTERVIEWER. What is your question please?

WOMAN 1. My question is, have you ever seen steak on the
menu of a really third-rate hotel because in my experience
that's very unusual.

YOU. Well, um, not personally.

WOMAN 1. Right. Perhaps next time it might be worth doing a bit more research, have you ever tried Trip Advisor?

INTERVIEWER. Another question. Yes, over there, black overcoat, roots need touching up.

WOMAN 2. I'd like to say thanks for being brave enough to write the poem.

YOU. Thank you.

WOMAN 2. And of course for going through such an unpleasant experience so we could share in it without having to have it ourselves.

YOU. Actually, I didn't – not everything I write is real.

WOMAN 2. What, so you made *everything* up, the clanging radiator, the salesman as well as the steak?

YOU. Well of course I've heard radiators make funny noises before, although not necessarily in a hotel with one star.

WOMAN 2. What about the salesman?

YOU. I think I'll leave that to your imagination.

WOMAN 2. But you're the one with the authentic voice, I think it's fair enough to want to know exactly how authentic, don't you?

INTERVIEWER. Question, person right at the back, aisle seat, crossed legs, evident depression.

WOMAN 3. Do you worry that you're sending out a negative message to older women about how depressing ageing is?

YOU. Well… that's the role of writing, I think, and art in general, I mean to explore what is uncomfortable about life –

WOMAN 3. But couldn't she have been a scientist or something, someone who'd done something significant and commendable so her life wasn't such a waste?

YOU. How do we know her life was a waste?

WOMAN 3. If she's picking up bald men in hotel bars at her age we could hardly say she'd made a success of it.

INTERVIEWER. Question? Yes, elderly woman with huge handbag, cataracts, face powder of a shade that in no way matches any human skin I've ever seen.

YOU. Sorry, can I go back to the last point – I think there's a slight confusion here about the meaning of authenticity. Writing is an act of imagination, after all.

WOMAN 1. Yes but you are responsible for the character aren't you?

WOMAN 2. Yes we might expect you to be accurate at the very least.

WOMAN 3. Write what you know, isn't that what the experts say?

WOMAN 2. Exactly, and what about this salesman?

YOU. The character in the poem dies of a heart attack in a cheap hotel.

INTERVIEWER. Yes, your point being?

YOU. If I had died in a cheap hotel room I wouldn't have been able to write the poem. As you can all see, I'm still very much alive. Any other questions before we break for a plastic cup of – I speak from experience – cheap warm overly sweet white wine?

The Fifth Big Question

You're seventy-five. You're with your granddaughter, who is five. You're watering your plants. (Your granddaughter is not present in the scene.)

YOU. Aren't you going to help Granny water the geraniums?

Short pause.

Oh, you'd rather read your storybook.

Short pause.

I'm not sure. How do *you* think it ends?

Short pause.

Yes, why not ask Rabbit. That's a good idea.

Short pause.

He doesn't want to say? That's all right. It'll be more of a surprise this way.

Woman Not On the Balcony

You're seventy-nine. You're being taken around a retirement show home.

ESTATE AGENTS. Here it is

We'd like you to picture yourself, right here

On the balcony

Breeze in hair, glass of wine in hand

(And if you don't drink)

If you don't drink, a juice, something refreshing

You're looking down at the manicured communal gardens with the ornamental water feature

Wearing your, if I may say so, very fetching sunglasses

Yes aren't they cool

So you're here on your balcony

Or you're down in the gardens themselves

Or strolling back from your sunny office

(She's retired, it's the retirement package)

Sorry, first-time buyers' morning, I'm still catching up

You're strolling back from the farmer's market with a recyclable canvas bag full of locally sourced organic

Seasonal

Locally sourced organic seasonal produce

Up the tree-lined street full of independent boutique shops

And you take the elevator up to your fifth-floor apartment

You wave hello to your neighbours who've all been carefully sourced from a pool of like-minded applicants

You open the door and you walk inside and you bask in the space and the light

Now how would that make you feel?

Because this choice, this purchase, is all about YOU

I won't ask your age, we'd never do that

But let's assume you're somewhere in your seventh decade

By the way would you like a chair?

(We already offered her the chair)

And as you know the seventh decade is all about YOU

Your kids have grown up, you've enjoyed a long and successful career

You've learned some hard lessons, you've made some mistakes

But the pressure's finally off

Financially, emotionally, physically, you can let go

And live how YOU'VE always wanted

See these fittings, the fixtures

All carefully sourced and copied from international artisans

Did we mention the pool?

Yes, the underground pool

It's open twenty-four hours a day

And if you're not comfortable being seen in a swimming costume which would be totally understandable you can do a keep-fit class in the gym which is fully staffed and monitored by permanent security cameras

Pause.

Well?

Any thoughts?

YOU *laugh.*

All right?

Madam?

YOU. Sorry, it's just... I've just seen myself clearly for the first time in my life

ESTATE AGENTS. What did we tell you?

Here on the balcony

Wine, breeze, sunglasses

Waving at your neighbour

YOU. No, that's not me. Not here. Not on the balcony

ESTATE AGENTS. In the kitchen, then, with the fittings

In the gardens, running your fingers through the fountain

YOU. No. Not in the kitchen or the garden. Not in the apartment

ESTAGE AGENTS. Where, then?

YOU. At home, in my own flat. With my clothes in the wardrobe and my food from the supermarket and my difficult neighbour and the boxes of photographs I still haven't sorted

ESTATE AGENTS. But this woman on the balcony –

YOU. I can see her perfectly. She just isn't me. I shouldn't waste any more of your time

YOU *smile at them and leave.*

ESTATE AGENTS. Senile

Cracked

Like her sunglasses

Cheap, that's why

Fake, from the market

Oh well

Who's up next?

Butterfly

You're in your mid-eighties. You're sitting on a chair.

YOU. Tired, suddenly

Birds

So clear, like rainwater

Make a good poem that

Nothing epic

I'm done with epics

Nice to just sit here and look at my little garden

Sun on my face

Rest the old legs

I'd miss it, this garden

You do miss things

Blackbirds

Eye contact

Those games we played, peasant girls, such fun

My animals

The way she'd lift my hair off the pillow so she could put her face closer to mine

There was that lovely pub with the carvery, it's closed now

But they're not important

Not worthy of a story

Quite a relief, really

Look – a butterfly

Ah. It's already gone

Epilogue

You're sitting in a waiting room, reading a celebrity magazine.

MAGAZINE. Died on a chair

   Favourite spot to

   Alone but serene

   With no regrets or

   Will was in order

   Family alerted

   Cupboards organised

   Won an award for

   Will be missed by

   Worthy send-off

   Hearts she touched on a regular basis

   Some OFFICIALS *enter with clipboards. They carry a balloon on a string and a receptacle full of items – it could be a box, a trolley, a bin liner. They address* YOU *directly.*

OFFICIALS. Welcome

   Welcome

   Welcome

   We hope it's been comfortable so far?

   Just to let you know you're completely safe here

   There's no agenda, just a few formalities, nothing too taxing

   And you can stop us at any point with pertinent questions

   Any pertinent questions so far?

   YOU *shake your head.*

   Good, shall we start the assessment?

The OFFICIALS *start to remove the items from the receptacle. The items should include one prop from every scene in the play. They briefly examine each one before putting it back into the receptacle. They make notes on their clipboards.*

Life well lived

Check

Positive influence

Check

Family, friends

Check

Choices, losses

Check

Loved, worked, felt

Check

Listened, fought, laughed

Check

Left, earned, heard

Check

Thought, tried, gave

Check

They close the receptacle.

Good

Lovely

Well done

YOU. Excuse me

OFFICIALS. Yes?

YOU. So it does all add up then?

OFFICIALS. They all ask that

It's not for us to say

They stand YOU *up and brush* YOU *down. They tie the balloon to your wrist.*

Just to clarify, so we don't seem careless, what we really mean is that the end result is of no real consequence to us

In the same way that a butterfly is of no consequence to a chair

Things are not naturally related, you see

Is it you and your colleagues who make those connections

You're very good at it

Very

But we are here to disconnect you

Lovingly

To reduce you to an essence that is easier to recycle so we can send you back

Everything clear so far?

YOU. Yes, I suppose so – yes

They walk YOU *into a new space.*

OFFICIALS. Off you go then and best of luck

It's bound to be different this time around though some of it might seem familiar

The big questions, we mean

The beginnings, middles, endings, et cetera

Still not to worry, it's all a work-in-progress

And don't forget you're welcome to draw your own conclusions

Ready?

YOU *nod. An* OFFICIAL *takes out a pin and pops the balloon. As it bangs – lights off.*

The End.

www.nickhernbooks.co.uk

facebook.com/nickhernbooks

twitter.com/nickhernbooks